3,—

TO
LOVE
A CAT

TO
LOVE
A CAT

Colleen Stanley Bare
Color photographs by the author

Dodd, Mead & Company   New York

To Vernice

Acknowledgments

Almond Joy Cattery, Vernice Lueth; *Bru Cattery,* De-layne Nance; Dorothy Crompton; Hannah Nance; Eileen Oesau; Kent and Jayne Olson; Ann and Robert Smith; Betty Tarone; and Joyce and Richard Welch.

Library of Congress Cataloging-in-Publication Data

Bare, Colleen Stanley.
    To love a cat.
    Summary: Introduces various kinds of cats and the care
they need to remain healthy and happy.
    I. Cats—Juvenile literature. [I. Cats] I. Title.
SF445.7.B37 1986   636.8   86-2156
ISBN 0-396-08834-1

There are
many
kinds
of cats:

Long-haired
cats,

short-haired
cats,

tiny, newborn kitten-cats,
old, sleepy, slow cats.

Show cats,

alley cats,

bushy-tailed,

skinny-tailed,
no-tailed cats.

Black cats,
white cats,
blue, brown,
cream,
lilac, red,
silver,
and multicolored cats.

Outdoor cats,
indoor cats,

out-and-in
and in-and-out
cats.

9

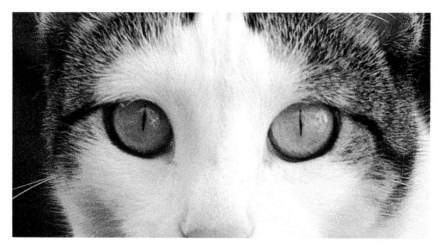

Green-eyed cats,
    orange-eyed cats,
blue, gray, copper, hazel,
and yellow-eyed cats.

Cats, cats, many
kinds of cats,
and their needs
are all the same....

Water and food every day

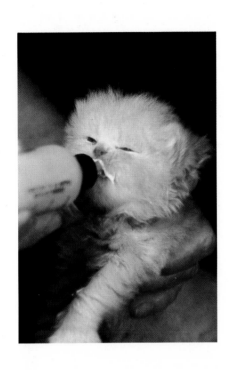

Mother's milk for
newborn kittens,
which may not
be enough.

Prepared cat foods,
milk for cats
that like milk,
and, sometimes,
people food—beef, chicken,
cooked eggs, cottage cheese.

A safe, cozy bed

A cardboard box,
a cat-on-the-go
carrier,

wire cages for
show cats,

baskets, baskets,
baskets,

14

and, cats' choices—sofas,
chairs, humans' beds,
and laps.

Handling with care

Tender, newborn baby cats
soon become big, grown-up cats,

but must be handled very gently

without dropping,
stepping on,
lying on,
tail pulling,
poking,
pinching,
punching,
squeezing,
or teasing.

Grooming and cleaning

Cats wash themselves and their kittens,

but still need

a litter box,

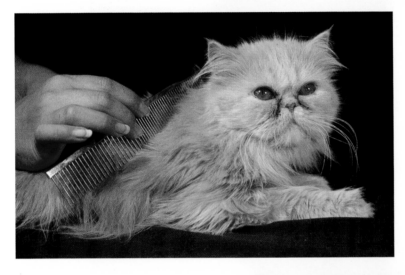

combing,

nail clipping,
ear cleaning.

Even a clean cat can become a
   dirty cat,
or a flea-bitten cat,
and need a bath.

The first rinse,

the shampoo,

the second
rinse,

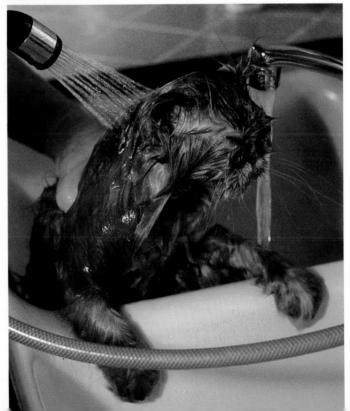

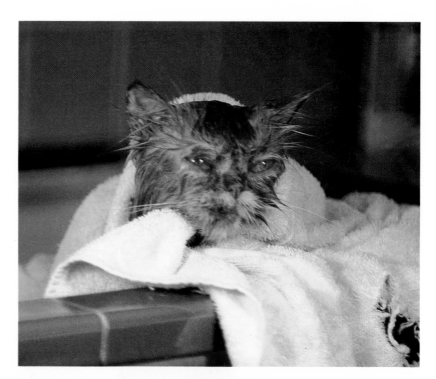

drying,

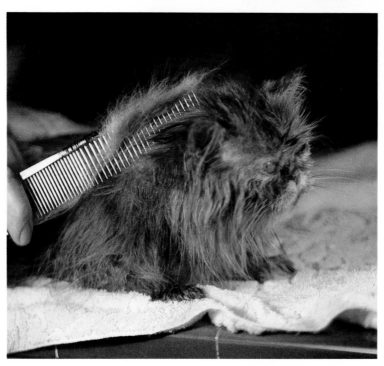

combing.

22

A playful cat likes toys

People toys,

cat toys,

hide-and-seek toys,

a scratching post for
playing and scratching.

A cat needs someone to understand its cat-talk

Meow,
meow,
meow,

or mew,
mew,
mew,

28

may mean, "Let me out,
let me in,
I am hungry,
I am hot,
I am cold,
I am scared,
I am sick,"
or even, "Help me, I am hurt!"

But happy cats purr, purr, purr, purr.

A cat is independent, beautiful, curious, warm, clever, playful, smart, and will reward your care with love.